HOW DO YOU LOOK LIKE YOU?

A SCIENCE BOOK ABOUT GENETICS

written by dr. victoria rea, phd
illustrated by srimalie bassani

T0191277

Have you ever looked in the mirror and wondered how you look like you? We may all have some similar features, but some things are special and only apply to us. Why do you have green eyes? Why do you have brown hair? How did you get your dimples!? It's all about genetics!

HOW DO YOU LOOK THE WAY YOU DO?

Did your mom give a drawing to the doctor before you were born?

You look like you because of your genes! Genes are the little bits of information inside your cells. Every living thing on planet Earth has genes inside their cells—animals, plants, and even fungus!

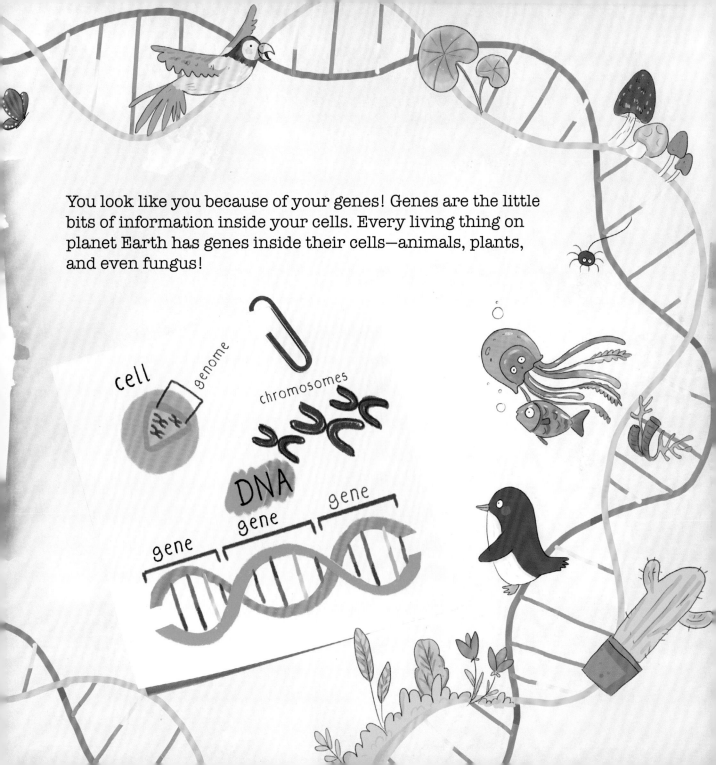

cell

genome

chromosomes

DNA

gene

gene

gene

Genes are like a set of instructions that tell your body what to do and how to look. Every gene has a different instruction for a different job in your body. The instructions are like a recipe for different physical traits that you have, such as curly hair or dimples.

BIG BOOK OF GENETIC RECIPES

Putting all your genes together makes one big recipe book for how you look like you!

RECIPE FOR LUCAS
INGREDIENTS

blue eyes

small ears

straight, red hair

pointed nose

HOW DO YOU GET YOUR GENES?

Are they shipped in from outer space?

Genes don't come from outer space;
genes come from your parents!

GENETIC FAMILY TREE

maternal grandmother

maternal grandfather

paternal grandmother

paternal grandfather

mom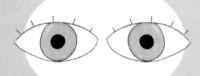

dad

me

Half of your genes come from one parent and half come from the other parent. That's why most people end up looking a little bit like both of their parents.

We've all got a jumbled mix of genes and traits from our parents!

Genes are made of strings of DNA and squeezed SUPER tightly into packages called chromosomes. Genes are so tiny that you can fit all 20,000 of them into 23 matching pairs of chromosomes inside a single cell.

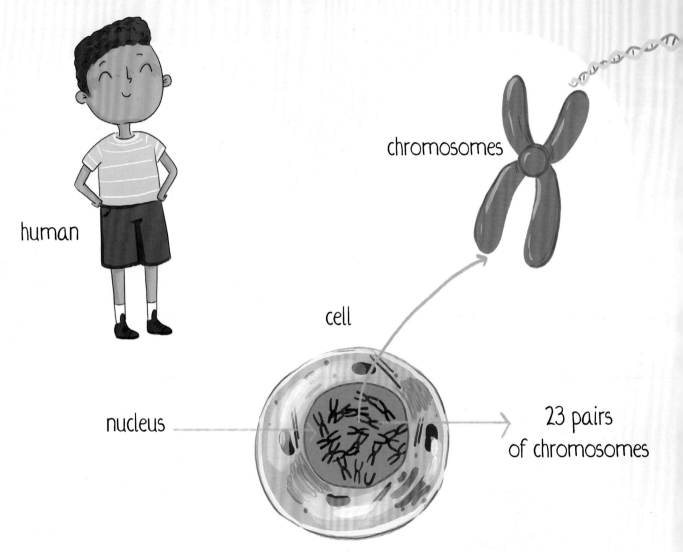

human

chromosomes

cell

nucleus

23 pairs
of chromosomes

FUN FACT
DNA molecules are in a shape called a double helix. It looks like this!

Let's go to the moon and beyond!

segment of data

We can't see DNA with our own eyes, but we have a lot of it. If you unraveled all the DNA in all the chromosomes in all your cells, you would have a string long enough to make 150,000 trips to the moon and back!

HOW DO YOU GET YOUR HAIR COLOR?

Do fairies paint it on your head every night when you go to sleep?

It would be pretty fun to have fairies visit you every night, but you don't need them to paint on your hair color because that comes from your parents too!

FUN FACT

You get 23 chromosomes from your mother and 23 chromosomes from your father!

Hair color is a trait that you inherit. Both parents pass down a gene for hair color, and then your body combines both instructions.

If one parent has brown hair and the other has blond hair, chances are you will have brown hair! That's because brown hair color is a dominant trait. It's sort of like the instructions for brown hair are in capital letters. So even if you have genes for both hair colors (brown from one parent and blond from the other), your hair will probably still be brown. Think about it like playing rock, paper, scissors. Just like paper beats rock, brown hair beats blond hair!

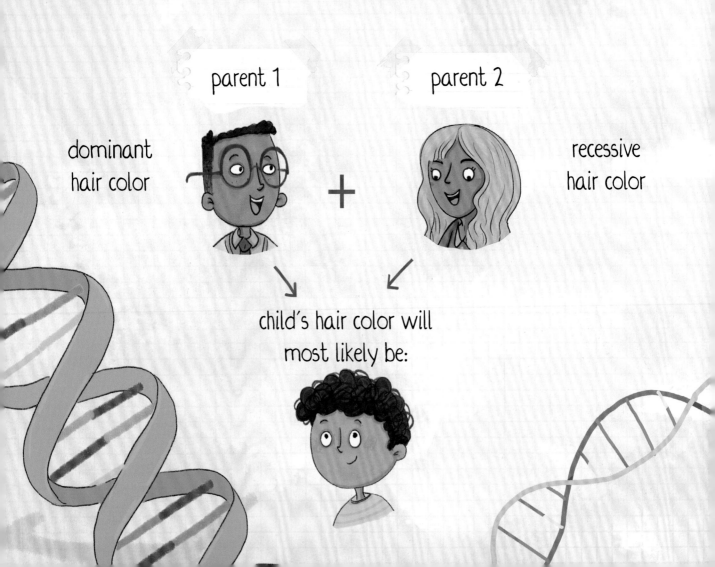

parent 1

parent 2

dominant hair color

recessive hair color

+

child's hair color will most likely be:

parent 1 + parent 2

child

If BOTH parents have blond hair, then you will probably have blond hair too. Since they both have blond hair, there's no competition from brown hair instructions. Consider it a tie!

GENETICS

HOW DO SOME PEOPLE GET FRECKLES AND OTHERS DON'T?

Are they secretly drawing them on with a marker every day?

No way! Freckles are special!

Very funny!

Mutations are a change in the order of the nucleotide bases in DNA. It can change the type of proteins a cell produces, for example having freckles or no freckles.

Whether or not you have freckles, it is important to wear sunscreen while outside to protect against skin damage.

Freckles are the result of a mutation in the MC1R gene. This gene is the recipe that tells your body how to make a tan. Everyone gets the MC1R gene from their parents, but some people have a mutation in this gene. Mutations mean that the gene doesn't work quite right. But not to worry! The mutated version of this gene just means that you only tan in certain places, such as the tiny little dots that we call freckles!

Have you put on sunscreen yet?

Mutations can be good or bad. They happen when there is a mistake in the DNA, kind of like a typo in the recipe. Sometimes it means that the gene is totally broken. Think about accidentally making nachos with BEES instead of nachos with CHEESE. That would be a VERY different recipe!

Some mistakes just mean the recipe will only be a little bit different, like putting ice cream on your cake when you're supposed to put icing.

Captain Unbreakable!

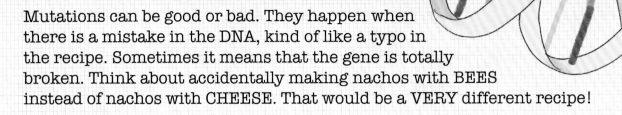

MORE EXAMPLES OF MUTATIONS:

UNBREAKABLE BONES

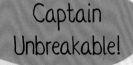

LRP5 is the gene that tells your body how dense your bones should be. A mutation in this gene makes your bones stronger than most people. The mutated form of this gene makes your bones so dense that they're actually really hard to break!

SUPER TASTERS

TAS2R38 is the gene that's responsible for how your body responds to bitter tastes. People with a mutation in this gene are called super tasters! The mutation makes them more sensitive to bitter foods, so they taste bitter foods more intensely. These people probably don't like the taste of Brussels sprouts, chocolate, or coffee.

Your gene mutation is no excuse not to eat your vegetables!

SHORT SLEEPERS

Sleep is really important. Most of us feel crummy if we don't get a full night's sleep. But there are some lucky people who are just fine with only a few hours of sleep a night! These people have a mutation in a gene called hDEC2 that's responsible for sleep-wake cycles. It means that their body naturally needs less sleep.

I only need 3 hours of sleep and I can even do it standing up!

HOW DO YOU GET TO BE AS TALL AS YOU ARE?

Does a team of tug-of-war champions stretch you out while you sleep?

(We promise that's not how!)

Height is a trait you get from your parents... mostly. The instructions for height come from lots of different genes, so there's a lot of variation that can happen with so much information contributing to one trait.

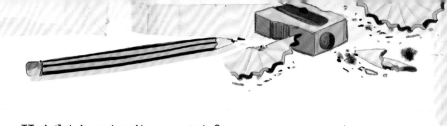

You have grown since I saw you!

Your genes will only tell your body how tall you CAN be, not how tall you WILL be.

Basically, your genes give the instructions for your full height potential, but there are other factors, such as what you eat, how much you sleep, and how much you exercise, that affect how tall you will eventually grow to be.

There are plenty of other times that genes work in combination with other factors to shape how you look and how your body grows. In addition to the genes you get from your parents, you also have traits that you get from your environment, for example an accent or a skill. Those acquired traits work together with your inherited genes to make you who you are.

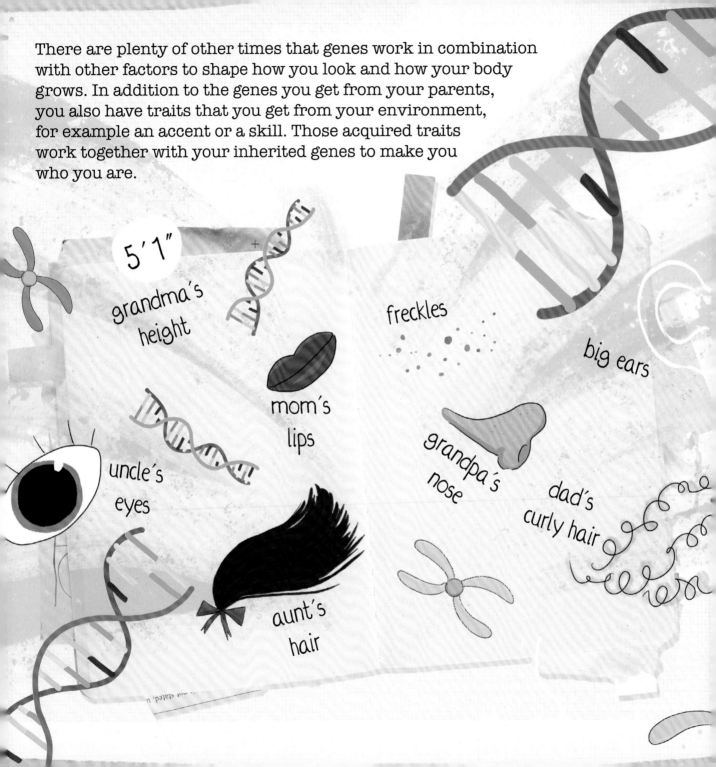

5' 1"

grandma's height

freckles

big ears

mom's lips

grandpa's nose

uncle's eyes

dad's curly hair

aunt's hair

HOW DO MY GENES MAKE ME LOOK DIFFERENT THAN MY BROTHER OR SISTER?

Well, your parents have variations of each gene and every time they have a new baby, it's like rolling the dice for every gene.

Let's see who I will look like!

Let's play rock, paper, scissors to see whose hair our baby gets!

I hope they have my hair!

A = dominant hair color

a = recessive hair color

I know what you're thinking: my traits come from my parents and my sibling has the same parents...why don't we look the same?!

The same way your parents each gave YOU a set of genes, your parents each got a set from THEIR parents. When you were born, you got a random mix of genes from each parent. When your brother or sister was born, they also got a random mix of the same genes. But just like rolling dice, you don't get the same result every time!

You could have received the brown hair gene from your mom, which really came from her mom, but your sister could have received the blond hair gene from your mom that came from her dad.

Think of how many combinations that could make! While you probably look similar to your siblings, not every characteristic or trait will be the exact same.

It's cool that we share the same genes as all living creatures!

With so many genes having to control so many things in our bodies, it's a wonder we're not all just piles of mush! It takes a lot of instructions to make our bodies work properly. Most of our genes are just instructions on how to be a living thing! This means we're actually very similar to all the living things around us.

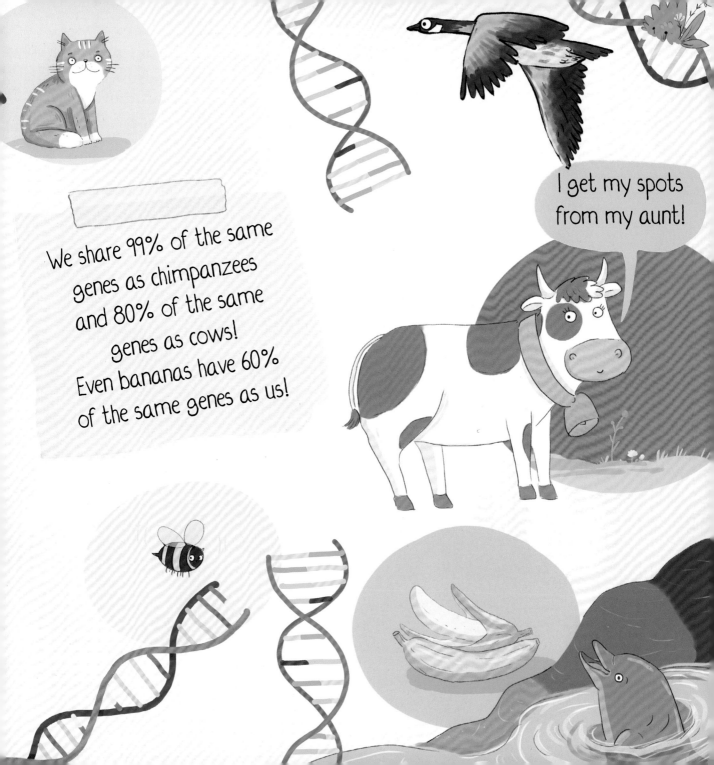

We share 99% of the same genes as chimpanzees and 80% of the same genes as cows! Even bananas have 60% of the same genes as us!

I get my spots from my aunt!

INHERITED V. ACQUIRED TRAITS

You've learned a lot about inheriting traits. But not all traits are inherited. Some traits we develop on our own as we grow up. Those are called acquired traits. Read below to learn about some traits that are inherited and some traits that are acquired.

FRECKLES

Some people *inherit* the tendency to develop freckles, which are small, flat, and tan or light-brown spots on the skin.

EYE COLOR

The color of your eyes is usually *inherited* from your parents.

HAIR COLOR

Like eye color, the color of your hair is often *inherited* from your parents.

DIMPLES

Dimples, those cute little indents when you smile, can be an *inherited* trait.

LANGUAGE

The language or languages you speak are *acquired* through learning and exposure.

SKILLS

Abilities such as playing a musical instrument, drawing, or playing a sport are *acquired* through practice and training.

HOBBIES

Whether you enjoy activities like reading, painting, or playing video games is an *acquired* preference.

ACCENTS

The way you speak is *acquired* based on the language and culture around you.

TASTE PREFERENCES

Likes and dislikes for certain foods are often *acquired* through exposure and personal experiences.

TRAIT OR TRADE

Test your skills in interpreting traits with your friends! This game works best with four players.

What you need:

- 2 sheets of paper
  (cut into 12 pieces each)
- scissors
- 1 sheet of paper or whiteboard
  for every player
- markers
- large bowl

How to play:

1. Divide the small pieces of paper evenly among all the players (for four players each person should have six). Then make sure each player has a piece of paper or whiteboard and a marker.

2. Each player will write one trait on each of their small pieces of paper. All of the traits must be something you can see on someone's face. Choose one trait for eyes, one for nose, one for ears, one for hair, one for mouth, and one of your choosing. Use these as examples: wears glasses, green eyes, red hair, freckles, large nose, large ears, etc.

3. Once each player has filled out their pieces of paper, drop them into the bowl.

4. Have each player draw a large oval on their remaining piece of paper or whiteboard. This will be their face.

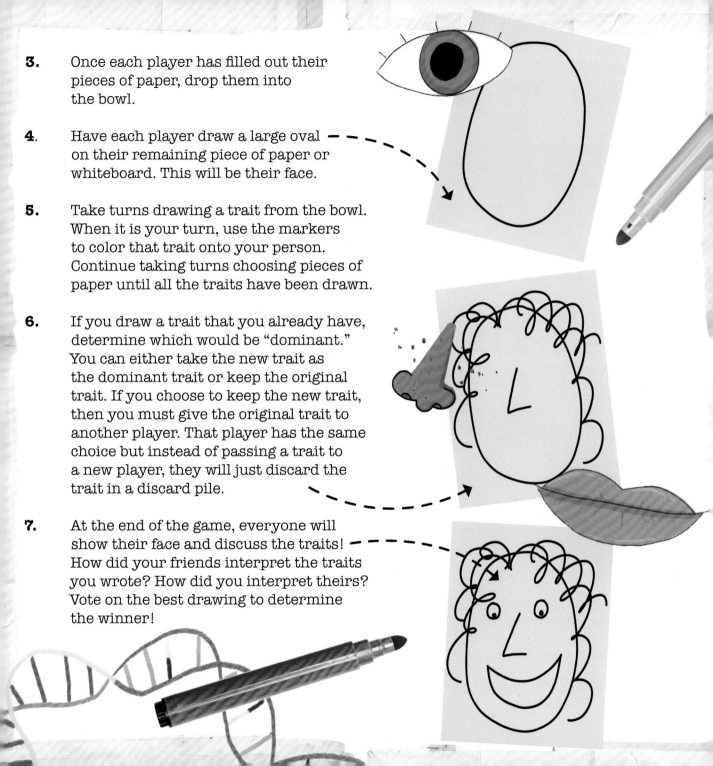

5. Take turns drawing a trait from the bowl. When it is your turn, use the markers to color that trait onto your person. Continue taking turns choosing pieces of paper until all the traits have been drawn.

6. If you draw a trait that you already have, determine which would be "dominant." You can either take the new trait as the dominant trait or keep the original trait. If you choose to keep the new trait, then you must give the original trait to another player. That player has the same choice but instead of passing a trait to a new player, they will just discard the trait in a discard pile.

7. At the end of the game, everyone will show their face and discuss the traits! How did your friends interpret the traits you wrote? How did you interpret theirs? Vote on the best drawing to determine the winner!

GLOSSARY

Acquired Traits – traits you develop throughout your life from your environment

Cell – the smallest building block of life that makes up all living things

Chromosomes – the tiny threadlike structures in the cell that carry all the instructions (genes) for making a living thing

Dominant Gene – a strong trait that can overrule a recessive gene

Genetics – the study of how traits and instructions are passed from parents to their children

Genes – these are the instructions that determine which traits are passed down from parents to children; they exist inside the cells that make up all living things

Genome – the genetic material found inside chromosomes that make up all living things

Inherited Traits – traits that are passed down to you through your DNA from your parents

Maternal – describes traits that come from your mom's side of the family

Mutation – a change or mistake in a gene

Nucleus – the control center of the cell where your chromosomes are

Paternal – describes traits that come from your dad's side of the family

Recessive Gene – a weaker trait or instruction that can be hidden by a dominant gene

Single Cell – the simplest form of life; made up of just one tiny cell

Traits – the special things that make you look and act the way you do